THE Pointless Book 2

CONTINUED BY ALFIE DEYES
FINISHED BY YOU

RUNNING PRESS
PHILADELPHIA · LONDON

TEXT © ALFIE DEYES
ALL IMAGES © BLINK PUBLISHING, EXCEPT PAGE 14 AND 19 © SHUTTERSTOCK
DESIGNED BY EMILY ROUGH, BLINK PUBLISHING

FIRST PUBLISHED IN THE UK IN 2015 BY BLINK PUBLISHING AN IMPRINT OF THE BONNIER PUBLISHING GROUP

FIRST PUBLISHED IN THE UNITED STATES IN 2015 BY RUNNING PRESS BOOK PUBLISHERS
A MEMBER OF THE PERSEUS BOOKS GROUP

BOOKS PUBLISHED BY RUNNING PRESS ARE AVAILABLE AT SPECIAL DISCOUNTS FOR BULK PURCHASES
IN THE UNITED STATES BY CORPORATIONS, INSTITUTIONS, AND OTHER ORGANIZATIONS. FOR MORE
INFORMATION, PLEASE CONTACT THE SPECIAL MARKETS DEPARTMENT AT THE PERSEUS BOOKS GROUP,
2300 CHESTNUT STREET, SUITE 200, PHILADELPHIA, PA 19103, OR CALL (800) 810-4145, EXT. 5000,
OR E-MAIL SPECIAL.MARKETS@PERSEUSBOOKS.COM.

ISBN 978-0-7624-5920-9
LIBRARY OF CONGRESS CONTROL NUMBER: 2014948505

9   8   7   6   5   4   3   2
DIGIT ON THE RIGHT INDICATES THE NUMBER OF THIS PRINTING

RUNNING PRESS BOOK PUBLISHERS
2300 CHESTNUT STREET
PHILADELPHIA, PA 19103-4371

VISIT US ON THE WEB!
WWW.RUNNINGPRESS.COM

THE POINTLESS BOOK 2
APP

CRANK UP THE POINTLESSNESS WITH THE POINTLESS BOOK 2 APP AND DOWNLOAD EXCLUSIVE VIDEOS OF ALFIE! ACCESS THE FREE APP FROM ITUNES OR GOOGLE PLAY, POINT YOUR DEVICE AT THE PAGES THAT DISPLAY THE SPECIAL ICON, AND THE VIDEOS WILL BE REVEALED ON SCREEN. HERE YOU WILL GET THE CHANCE TO WATCH VIDEOS OF ALFIE MAKING FULL ENGLISH CUPCAKES, DRAWING BLINDFOLDED, PLAYING SODA PONG AND MANY, MANY MORE FUN AND POINTLESS CHALLENGES! USING THE AUGMENTED REALITY TECHNOLOGY YOU CAN SHOW OFF YOUR CREATIVITY BY DESIGNING YOUR OWN POINTLESS CUP, BALL AND TRAINER! YOU CAN ALSO TAKE YOUR OWN PHOTOS WITH ALFIE AND SHARE THEM IN THE POINTLESS SELFIE BOOTH! THE APP INCLUDES EVEN MORE POINTLESS ACTIVITIES COMPLETED BY ALFIE, INCLUDING HIS FAVORITE WEIRD FOODS, HIS SECRET SUPER POWER AND HIS HILARIOUS CARTOON CHARACTER.

THE POINTLESS BOOK APP REQUIRES AN INTERNET CONNECTION TO BE DOWNLOADED, AND CAN BE USED ON IPHONE, IPAD OR ANDROID DEVICES. FOR LINKS TO DOWNLOAD THE APP AND FURTHER INFORMATION, VISIT WWW.RUNNINGPRESS.COM/THEPOINTLESSBOOKS

THIS BOOK BELONGS TO:

SIGNED BY ALFIE:

DRAW YOUR FAVORITE FOOD...

HAVE YOU EVER...

SEE ALFIE'S CHOICES

Y   N

BEEN ON A ROAD TRIP? ☐ ☐

PEED IN THE SEA? ☐ ☐

PRETENDED TO BE A MANNEQUIN IN A SHOP? ☐ ☐

CHEATED WHILE PLAYING A GAME? ☐ ☐

FALLEN ASLEEP ON PUBLIC TRANSPORT? ☐ ☐

GONE WITHOUT SHOWERING FOR OVER A WEEK? ☐ ☐

STAYED AWAKE ALL NIGHT? ☐ ☐

EATEN FOOD THAT HAS FALLEN ON THE FLOOR? ☐ ☐

SPIED ON YOUR NEIGHBOURS? ☐ ☐

MADE A PRANK PHONE CALL? ☐ ☐

SENT SOMEONE THE WRONG TEXT? ☐ ☐

HAD A BAD HAIRCUT? ☐ ☐

DRAW YOUR DREAM TREEHOUSE...

$ WHAT WOULD YOU $
DO IF YOU WON A
MILLION DOLLARS?

_____

_____

_____

_____

_____

_____

_____

_____

_____

_____

_____

_____

_____

_____

_____

_____

_____

_____

THE BLINDFOLD MAKE-UP CHALLENGE

WATCH ALFIE'S MAKE-UP CHALLENGE

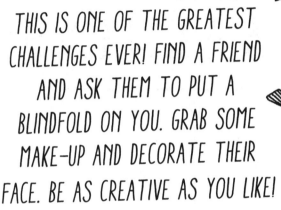

THIS IS ONE OF THE GREATEST CHALLENGES EVER! FIND A FRIEND AND ASK THEM TO PUT A BLINDFOLD ON YOU. GRAB SOME MAKE-UP AND DECORATE THEIR FACE. BE AS CREATIVE AS YOU LIKE!

TWEET YOUR ATTEMPTS TO #POINTLESSMAKEUP

WARNING LABEL!

IF YOU HAD A WARNING LABEL WHAT WOULD IT BE?
(FOR EXAMPLE: DON'T WAKE ME UP BEFORE 10AM!)

WARNING!

TODAY'S

DATE: _____

FIRST THOUGHT: _____

BREAKFAST: _____

BEST MOMENT: _____

FAVORITE TV SHOW: _____

TREAT: _____

BOOK: _____

CHALLENGE: _____

PAIR OF SHOES: _____

GOSSIP: _____

BEST CONVERSATION: _____

JOKE: _____

ACHIEVEMENT: _____

BEST TEXT: _____

GOOD DEED: _____

THE POINTLESS PHONE CHALLENGE

IT'S TIME FOR THE POINTLESS PHONE CHALLENGE! THIS GAME IS A LOT OF FUN AND CAN BE ABSOLUTELY HILARIOUS! HERE'S HOW TO PLAY:

1. IN THE BOXES BELOW, WRITE SIX OF THE MOST OUTRAGEOUS THINGS YOU'VE EVER HEARD.

2. GRAB YOUR MOBILE PHONE AND OPEN YOUR CONTACTS.

3. FIND A FRIEND AND ASK THEM TO DO THE SAME WITH THEIR MOBILE PHONE.

4. TAKE IT IN TURNS TO SCROLL THROUGH YOUR CONTACTS LIST WITHOUT LOOKING. WHEN THE OTHER PLAYER SAYS 'STOP', YOU HAVE TO CALL OR TEXT YOUR CONTACT, SAYING/WRITING ONE OF THE LINES BELOW...

INVENT A CATCHPHRASE

EVERYONE HAS A CATCHPHRASE THESE DAYS. TRY TO THINK OF ONE BASED ON YOUR NAME OR YOUR FRIEND'S NAME. IT'S EASIER THAN YOU THINK!

OH MY DEYES!

_____

_____

_____

_____

_____

_____

_____

_____

_____

POINTLESS RIDDLES

HERE ARE A COUPLE OF BRAIN TEASERS FOR YOU TO SOLVE. WRITE THE ANSWERS IN THE SPACE PROVIDED:

1. I TRAVEL A LOT—IN FACT I'VE BEEN TO EVERY COUNTRY IN THE WORLD! I'M INVISIBLE BUT YOU CAN SOMETIMES SEE ME.

_____

2. HOW MANY SECONDS ARE IN ONE YEAR?

_____

3. WHAT GOES UP WHEN THE RAIN COMES DOWN?

_____

4. I'M AN ANCIENT INVENTION THAT ALLOWS YOU TO SEE THROUGH WALLS. WHAT AM I?

_____

MAKE UP A STORY USING THESE WORDS...

WORLD, PIZZA, FINGERNAIL, COMB, SLEEP, HILARIOUS, HAIR, TWEET, FRIENDS, FRECKLE

_____

_____

_____

_____

_____

_____

_____

_____

_____

_____

_____

_____

SCAN HERE

COMPLETE THE MAZE!

START

GRAB A PENCIL AND TRACE YOUR ROUTE THROUGH THE POINTLESS MAZE. BEGIN AT THE START POINT AND MAKE YOUR WAY THROUGH TO THE END WITHOUT LIFTING YOUR PENCIL OFF THE PAGE!

END

CURRENTLY I'M

READING: _____

WATCHING: _____

SINGING: _____

THINKING: _____

EATING: _____

WISHING: _____

WANTING: _____

NEEDING: _____

TEXTING: _____

DRINKING: _____

TWEETING: _____

WRITING: _____

LEARNING: _____

HOPING: _____

CALLING: _____

DON'T BREAK THE CHAIN

WATCH ALFIE IN ACTION

LET'S PLAY A GAME OF WORD ASSOCIATION. MATCH THE WORD TO THE PREVIOUS ONE WITHOUT STOPPING. HOW MANY WORDS CAN YOU DO IN ONE MINUTE?

RED

ROSE

SCENT

CANDLE

ROOM

DRAW YOUR DREAM HOUSE

FIVE CITIES I'D LIKE TO VISIT...

SCAN HERE TO SEE ALFIE'S TOP 5

1 _____

2 _____

3 _____

4 _____

5 _____

MY FANTASY DAY

8AM: _____

10AM: _____

12PM: _____

2PM: _____

4PM: _____

6PM: _____

8PM: _____

10PM: _____

MUFFIN IN A MUG

INGREDIENTS:

1 CUP OF FLOUR
1 TBSP BROWN SUGAR
1/2 TSP BAKING POWDER
1/8 TSP SALT
A PINCH OF CINNAMON
1/2 TBSP BUTTER
2 TBSP MILK
1-2 TBSP FROZEN BLUEBERRIES

1. CHOOSE A MUG. ADD THE FLOUR, BROWN SUGAR, BAKING POWDER, SALT, AND CINNAMON AND GIVE IT A GOOD MIX.

2. ADD THE BUTTER AND USE YOUR FINGERS TO SMOOSH IT ALL TOGETHER UNTIL ALL OF THOSE BUTTER CHUNKS HAVE DISAPPEARED.

3. ADD THE MILK INTO THE BUTTERY-FLOURY MIXTURE AND STIR UNTIL IT'S SMOOTH AND MOIST (DON'T WORRY IF IT LOOKS A BIT DRY, JUST ADD MORE MILK!). SCATTER THE BLUEBERRIES ON TOP AND PUSH THEM DOWN INTO THE MIXTURE.

4. PLACE YOUR MUG OF DELICIOUSNESS IN THE MICROWAVE AND COOK ON THE HIGHEST SETTING FOR TWO MINUTES.

5. ONCE YOU HEAR THE 'DING' TAKE THE MUG OUT, LET IT COOL THEN IT'S READY TO EAT!

POINTLESS OPPOSITES

EVERYTHING HAS AN OPPOSITE—YOU JUST NEED TO USE YOUR IMAGINATION. WHAT'S THE OPPOSITE OF A CUP? A SAUCER! WHAT'S THE OPPOSITE OF A DOG? A CAT! EVEN PEOPLE HAVE AN OPPOSITE—YOU JUST NEED TO BE CREATIVE. HERE ARE A FEW TO GET YOU STARTED:

AL-FIE DEYES   EARLY BIRD-FREE NIGHTS

TINIE TEMPAH   LARGE HAPPINESS

TAYLOR SWIFT   _____

LADY GAGA   _____

JAMIE OLIVER   _____

_____   _____

_____   _____

_____   _____

_____

DRAW A PICTURE...

...ONLY USING TRIANGLES

SCAN HERE
TO SEE
ALFIE'S
PICTURE

DRAW YOURSELF IN 50 YEARS...

POINTLESS PHOTOBOMB!

GRAB YOUR POINTLESS BOOK 2 AND TRY TO SNEAK INTO SOMEONE'S PICTURE. GOT ANY GREAT PHOTOBOMBS? TWEET THEM TO

#POINTLESSPHOTO

MAKE UP A POINTLESS SONG

EVERYONE HAS A SONG INSIDE THEM! GET CREATIVE AND PEN A POINTLESS TUNE. YOU CAN BASE IT ON A POPULAR SONG OR EVEN MAKE ONE UP FROM SCRATCH!

LEARN TO TALK SDRAWKCAB!

GNIKLAT SDRAWKCAB SI
ENO FO S'EFIL TSETAERG
STFIG. TSUJ ETARAPES EHT
SDROW OTNI SELBALLYS
DNA YAS TI KCIUQ! DNA
REBMEMER STNANOSNOC TA
EHT GNINNIGEB FO SDROW
ERA TNELIS!

MOONWALKING LESSON!

THERE'S A TIME AND A PLACE FOR A MOONWALK: WHEN YOU'RE ON THE DANCEFLOOR; WHEN YOU'RE WALKING TO THE STORES; WHEN YOU'RE LEAVING CLASS AFTER ACING AN EXAM. BUT NOT EVERYONE KNOWS HOW TO DO IT PROPERLY. HERE'S A LESSON ON LIFE'S GREATEST DANCE MOVE...

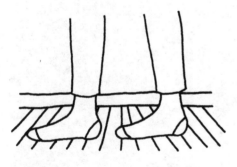

1. FIND A NICE OPEN SPACE (PREFERABLY A HARD WOODEN FLOOR).

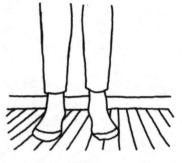

2. STAND AT ONE END OF THE ROOM WITH YOUR FEET SHOULDER-WIDTH APART.

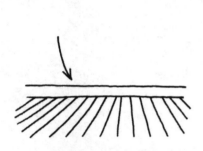

3. PLACE ONE FOOT IN FRONT OF THE OTHER.

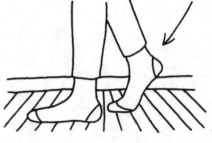

4. LIFT THE HEEL OF YOUR BACK FOOT OFF THE FLOOR.

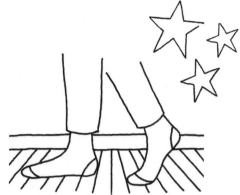

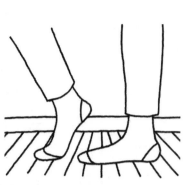

5. SLIDE YOUR FRONT FOOT ALONGSIDE YOUR BACK FOOT UNTIL IT'S BEHIND YOU.

6. ONCE YOUR SLIDING FOOT IS BEHIND YOU, SHIFT POSITION SO THE HEEL OF YOUR SLIDING FOOT IS OFF THE FLOOR AND THE HEEL OF YOUR STANDING FOOT IS FLAT.

7. REPEAT.

8. PUT ON 'BILLIE JEAN' AND SHOW YOUR FRIENDS.

VIDEO-MIME CHALLENGE

TWEET A VIDEO OF YOURSELF MIMING ALONG TO YOUR FAVORITE SONG TO

#POINTLESSMIME

FACE IMPRESSIONS

THERE ARE IMPRESSIONS AND THEN THERE ARE FACE IMPRESSIONS. USING ONE FACIAL EXPRESSION, DO AN IMPRESSION OF THE FOLLOWING ANIMALS...

HAPPY DOG

CONFUSED HORSE

SAD CAT

WORRIED PENGUIN

MAKE UP SOME MORE OF YOUR OWN!

ALFIE'S JUICE RECIPE

INGREDIENTS:

1 CUP OF BLACKBERRIES.
1 CUP OF BLUEBERRIES.
1 CUP OF RASPBERRIES.
1 TEASPOON OF HONEY.
1 CUP OF WATER.
SOME ICE CUBES!

METHOD:

1. FIRST, ADD ALL THE INGREDIENTS TO THE BLENDER AND BLEND UNTIL SMOOTH.

2. GRAB A GLASS, HOLD A STRAINER OVER IT AND POUR THE JUICE THROUGH IT.

3. POP A FEW LEFTOVER BERRIES ON TOP AND YOU'RE DONE!

NAMES IN A HAT

GRAB SOME FRIENDS (AND A COUPLE HATS!) FOR A GAME OF CHARADES—WITH A DIFFERENCE. HERE'S HOW YOU PLAY:

1. CUT OUT THE TABS BELOW AND DISTRIBUTE THREE TO EVERY PLAYER.

2. EACH FRIEND THEN WRITES THE NAME OF THREE FAMOUS PEOPLE OR CHARACTERS AND PLACES THE NAMES IN HAT ONE.

3. SPLIT THE GROUP INTO TWO TEAMS AND ONCE YOU'RE READY, NOMINATE ONE PERSON TO GO FIRST.

4. IN ROUND ONE THE PLAYER HAS 30 SECONDS TO DESCRIBE THE NAME USING CHARADES—NO TALKING, ONLY ACTING! WHEN HIS OR HER TEAM GUESSES THE CORRECT NAME, THE PLAYER PLACES THE CORRECT TAB INTO HAT TWO.

5. AFTER 30 SECONDS IT'S THE OTHER TEAM'S GO. MAKE SURE THAT THE FIRST TEAM KEEPS A TALLY OF HOW MANY NAMES THEY GUESSED.

6. ONCE ALL THE NAMES HAVE BEEN PICKED FROM HAT ONE IT'S TIME FOR ROUND TWO. IN THIS ROUND THE PLAYER HAS 30 SECONDS TO DESCRIBE THE FAMOUS PERSON OR CHARACTER WITHOUT SAYING THE NAME ON THE TAB.

7. AS WITH THE PREVIOUS ROUND, ONCE THE TEAM GUESSES THE CORRECT TAB, THE PLAYER PLACES THE PIECE OF PAPER BACK INTO HAT ONE. AND REMEMBER TO KEEP A POINTS TALLY!

8. ONCE ALL THE NAMES HAVE BEEN PICKED IT IS TIME FOR ROUND THREE. THIS TIME EACH PLAYER HAS TO DESCRIBE THE NAME OF THE FAMOUS PERSON OR CELEBRITY USING ONE WORD.

9. REPEAT THE PROCESS JUST LIKE THE PREVIOUS ROUNDS.

10. THE WINNING GROUP IS THE TEAM WITH THE MOST POINTS AT THE END OF THE GAME!

20 FACTS
ABOUT ME

SCAN HERE FOR ALFIE'S 20 FACTS

1. _____

2. _____

3. _____

4. _____

5. _____

6. _____

7. _____

8. _____

9. _____

10. _____

11. _____

12. _____

13. _____

14. _____

15. _____

16. _____

17. _____

18. _____

19. _____

20. _____

OPTICAL ILLUSIONS

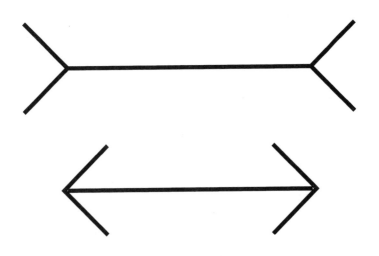

THE TOP LINE APPEARS LONGER THAN THE BOTTOM
ONE BUT IS ACTUALLY THE SAME LENGTH.

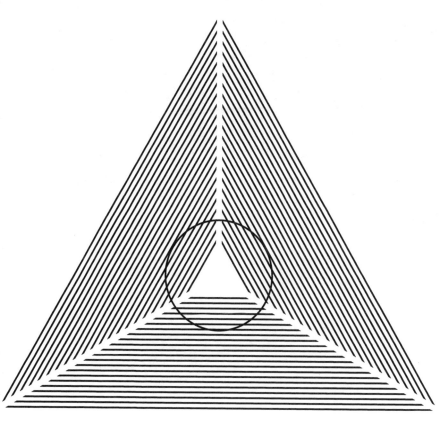

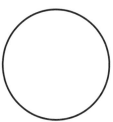

THE ROUND CIRCLE ON THE LINES IN THE TRIANGLE IS
IDENTICAL TO THE ONE BELOW.

PAPER PIZZA TOPPINGS

MMMM PIZZA. MAKE YOUR OWN USING THE CUT OUT TOPPINGS AND BASE BELOW. YOU CAN MAKE UP A NAME FOR YOUR CREATION TOO!

NAME:

DRAW A HORSE...

SCAN HERE TO SEE ALFIE'S HORSE

HOW WELL DO YOU KNOW YOUR BEST FRIEND?

WRITE DOWN THE ANSWERS TO THE QUESTIONS BELOW AND
HAND THEM TO YOUR FRIEND TO CORRECT...

1. WRITE DOWN THEIR PHONE NUMBER, FROM MEMORY!

2. WHAT IS THE NAME OF THEIR FIRST CRUSH?

3. WHAT IS THEIR FAVORITE FOOD?

4. WHAT IS THEIR MIDDLE NAME?

5. WHAT IS THEIR FAVORITE FILM?

6. LIST THREE THINGS THEY WOULD NEVER LEAVE HOME WITHOUT?

7. WHAT IS THEIR BIGGEST PET HATE?

8. WHAT IS THEIR DREAM JOB?

9. WHERE WOULD THEY MOST LIKE TO LIVE?

10. WHAT IS THEIR MOST EMBARRASSING MOMENT?

11. WHAT TOPPINGS WOULD THEY WANT ON THEIR PIZZA?

12. WHO IS THEIR FAVORITE YOUTUBER?

TRY NOT TO LAUGH CHALLENGE

FIND A FRIEND WHO YOU FIND PARTICULARLY FUNNY, SIT FACING EACH OTHER AND SEE HOW LONG IT TAKES BEFORE THEY CAN MAKE YOU LAUGH. RECORD YOUR PERSONAL BESTS BELOW...

PERSONAL BEST 1: _____

PERSONAL BEST 2: _____

PERSONAL BEST 3: _____

PERSONAL BEST 4: _____

PERSONAL BEST 5: _____

PERSONAL BEST 6: _____

WRITE YOUR OWN RECIPE

NAME: _____

INGREDIENTS: METHOD:

_____   _____
_____   _____
_____   _____
_____   _____
_____   _____
_____   _____
_____   _____
_____   _____
_____   _____
_____   _____
_____   _____
_____   _____
                  _____
                  _____
                  _____
                  _____
                  _____
                  _____
                  _____

WHAT DID IT TASTE LIKE?

_____
_____
_____

SECRET PAGE...

...FIND THE KEY TO UNLOCK THE BOX

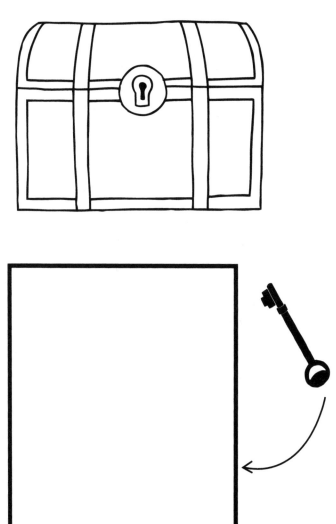

DRAW
SOMETHING THAT
REMINDS YOU OF...

YOUR BEST
FRIEND...

ALFIE DEYES...

YOUR MOM...

YOUR FAVORITE
SONG...

YOUR FAVORITE
MEMORY...

YOUR HOMETOWN...

HANG MAN

IT'S TIME FOR A CLASSIC GAME OF HANG MAN...

7 WAYS TO IMPROVE YOUR LIFE...

SCAN HERE TO SEE ALFIE'S CHOICES

1. _____

2. _____

3. _____

4. _____

5. _____

6. _____

7. _____

10 THINGS TO DO THIS SUMMER...

1. _____

2. _____

3. _____

4. _____

5. _____

6. _____

7. _____

8. _____

9. _____

10. _____

5 THINGS YOU WOULD CHANGE ABOUT THE WORLD

1. _____
_____
_____

2. _____
_____
_____

3. _____
_____
_____

4. _____
_____
_____

5. _____
_____
_____

THE BLINDFOLD DRAWING CHALLENGE

A MEERKAT

WITH A FRIEND DRAW THE FOLLOWING BLINDFOLDED...

SCAN HERE TO SEE ALFIE'S ATTEMPT

A FRIEND

SEASON THIS PAGE...

...WITH SALT AND PEPPER

SPECIAL WEEKEND DIARY

FRIDAY _____
_____
_____
_____
_____
_____
_____

SATURDAY _____
_____
_____
_____
_____
_____

SUNDAY _____
_____
_____
_____
_____

A DAY IN THE LIFE OF YOU...

DATE:

THE NUMBERS GAME

SPELL OUT THE NUMBERS—HOW FAR CAN YOU
GET BEFORE YOU REACH THE LETTER 'A'?

ONE

TWO

THREE

SHADOW PUPPETS

HAVE YOU EVER TRIED MAKING A SHADOW PUPPET ON THE WALL?
ALL YOU NEED IS A TORCH, A DARK ROOM AND A CLEAR SPACE UPON
WHICH TO PERFORM YOUR AMAZING PUPPETRY! HERE ARE A FEW
CREATURES TO GET YOU STARTED...

A CHICKEN

A SWAN

A BULL

A PARROT

A BUTTERFLY

A STAG

A DOG

A HORSE

A RABBIT

A SNAIL

IF YOU WERE THE OPPOSITE SEX WHAT WOULD YOUR NAME BE?

MALE

FEMALE

DESIGN YOUR OWN TRAINER

SCAN HERE TO SEE YOUR DESIGN

BRING OUT YOUR INNER-DESIGNER BY COLORING IN THIS TRAINER.

MAKE SURE YOU COLOR WITHIN THE LINES!

FORTUNE TELLER CHALLENGE

CHECK OUT THE FORTUNE TELLER CHALLENGE! USING THE INSTRUCTIONS BELOW AND ON THE PAGE OPPOSITE, CONSTRUCT YOUR OWN FORTUNE TELLER. DON'T FORGET TO ADD A FEW DARES TO YOUR FORTUNE TELLER TO MAKE IT EVEN MORE FUN!

1.

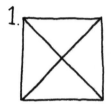

FOLD THE OPPOSITE CORNERS TOGETHER. UNFOLD SO YOU HAVE A SQUARE WITH A X CREASE.

2.

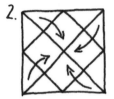

FOLD CORNERS INTO THE CENTRE SO POINTS MEET. TURNOVER AND FOLD TO THE CENTRE AGAIN.

3.

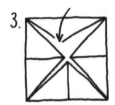

TURN YOUR SQUARE OVER AND FOLD EACH OF THE FOUR CORNERS TO THE CENTRE POINT AGAIN SO THAT YOUR SQUARE NOW STARTS TO LOOK LIKE THE DIAGRAM ABOVE.

4.

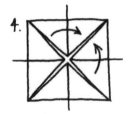

NOW FOLD IN HALF, UNFOLD AND FOLD AGAIN.

5.

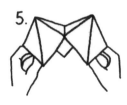

PUT YOUR FINGER AND THUMB UNDER THE FLAPS AND PUSH TOGETHER TO MAKE YOUR FORTUNE TELLER.

CUT OUT THE SQUARE ON THE DOTTED LINES!

1

2

8

3

THE
Pointless
Book 2

7

4

6

5

ADD COLOR HERE

ADD YOUR DARES HERE

FAVORITE WORDS

LIST YOUR FAVORITE WORDS HERE:

POINTLESS PATH PUZZLE

HELP NALA FIND HER WAY TO HER TASTY TREAT!

HOW MANY CLOTHES CAN YOU PUT ON IN ONE GO?

LIST WHAT YOU'RE WEARING HERE:

ONCE YOU'VE COMPLETED THE CHALLENGE TWEET A PICTURE TO #CLOTHESCHALLENGE

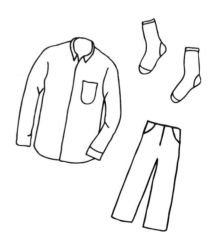

THE 'DO MORE OF WHAT MAKES YOU HAPPY' TRANSLATION PAGE!

THIS PAGE IS DEDICATED TO ALL OF ALFIE'S FOLLOWERS AROUND THE WORLD! HERE'S HIS FAVORITE PHRASE—DO MORE OF WHAT MAKES YOU HAPPY!—IN TEN DIFFERENT LANGUAGES. NAME THE LANGUAGE!

多做什么使你快乐!

_____

MACHEN SIE MEHR VON DEM, WAS DICH GLÜCKLICH MACHT!

_____

FARE DI PIÙ DI QUELLO CHE TI RENDE FELICE!

_____

Κάντε περισσότερα από ό, τι σε κάνει ευτυχισμένο!

_____

FAIRE PLUS DE CE QUI VOUS REND HEUREUX!

_____

HACER MÁS DE LO QUE TE HACE FELIZ!

_____

IF YOU COULD SPEAK ANOTHER LANGUAGE WHAT WOULD IT BE?

_____

WHAT'S YOUR POPSTAR NAME?

COUNTRIES A - Z

IN THE LIST BELOW, NAME A COUNTRY BEGINNING WITH
EVERY LETTER OF THE ALPHABET...

A

B

C

D

E

F

G

H

I

J

K

L

M

N

O

P

Q

R

S

T

U

V

W

X

Y

Z

WHAT'S YOUR SUPERHERO POWER?

SCAN TO SEE ALFIE'S CHOICE

SPIDERMAN CAN CLIMB WALLS. SUPERMAN CAN FLY. WHAT WOULD YOURS BE?

IF YOU WERE AN ANIMAL...

DRAW WHAT YOU WOULD BE:

APPLE BOBBING

 SCAN HERE TO SEE ALFIE'S ATTEMPTS

LET'S HAVE A GAME OF APPLE BOBBING! HERE'S HOW TO PLAY:

1. GRAB SIX APPLES.

2. GRAB A BIG BOWL OF WATER.

3. MARK EACH APPLE WITH THE NUMBERS '1' TO '6'.

4. PLACE THE APPLES IN THE BOWL.

5. FIND A FRIEND.

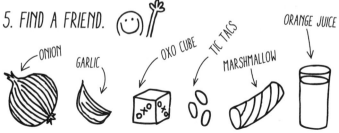

ONION   GARLIC   OXO CUBE   TIC TACS   MARSHMALLOW   ORANGE JUICE

6. FIND THREE THINGS YOU DON'T LIKE TO EAT—SUCH AS A BOUILLON CUBE, AN ONION AND A CLOVE OF GARLIC, AND THREE THINGS YOU LOVE TO EAT—SUCH AS A MARSHMALLOW, SOME TIC TACS AND A GLASS OF ORANGE JUICE. LABEL EACH ITEM NUMBERS '1' TO '6'.

7. TAKE IT IN TURNS TO FISH OUT THE APPLES WITHOUT USING YOUR HANDS. YOU THEN HAVE TO EAT OR DRINK THE ITEM THAT CORRESPONDS TO THE APPLE!

SNAKES AND LADDERS

THE AIM OF THE GAME IS TO BE THE FIRST PLAYER TO REACH SQUARE 90!

RULES OF PLAY:

1. EACH PLAYER ROLLS THE DICE. WHOEVER ROLLS THE HIGHEST NUMBER GETS TO PLAY FIRST.

2. PLAYER ONE, ROLL THE DICE AND MOVE FORWARD THAT NUMBER OF SPACES. IF YOU ROLL A 6 THEN YOU GET TO HAVE AN EXTRA TURN!

3. IF YOU LAND ON THE BASE OF A LADDER THEN YOU CAN CLIMB RIGHT UP TO THE TOP OF IT (HOORAY!) BUT IF YOU LAND ON THE HEAD OF A SNAKE YOU MUST SLIDE BACK DOWN TO ITS TAIL (UNLUCKY!). NOW PASS THE DICE ON TO THE NEXT PLAYER.

4. TO WIN THE GAME, ONE PLAYER MUST LAND EXACTLY ON SQUARE 90. IF YOU ROLL TOO HIGH THEN YOU HAVE TO MOVE BOTH FORWARDS AND BACKWARDS TO COMPLETE YOUR TURN. (FOR EXAMPLE, IF YOU ARE ON SQUARE 88 AND ROLL A 3, YOU MUST MOVE FORWARD TWO SPACES TO 90 AND THEN BACK ONE SPACE IN ORDER TO FULFIL THE THREE MOVES).

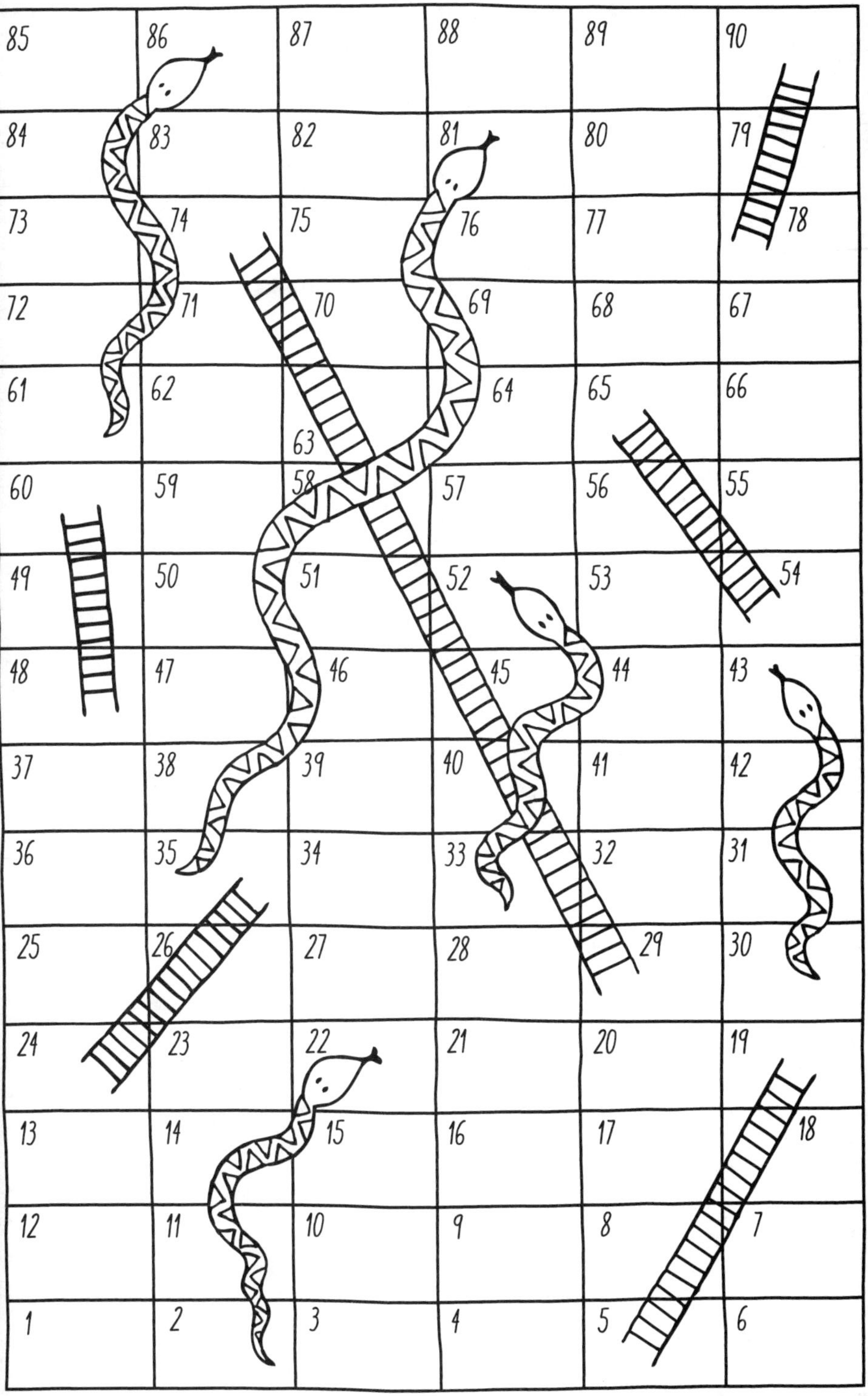
85 86 87 88 89 90
84 83 82 81 80 79
73 74 75 76 77 78
72 71 70 69 68 67
61 62 63 64 65 66
60 59 58 57 56 55
49 50 51 52 53 54
48 47 46 45 44 43
37 38 39 40 41 42
36 35 34 33 32 31
25 26 27 28 29 30
24 23 22 21 20 19
13 14 15 16 17 18
12 11 10 9 8 7
1 2 3 4 5 6

GET YOUR FRIENDS TO SIGN THIS PAGE

TONGUE TWISTERS

TRY SAYING THESE REALLY QUICKLY:

I SCREAM, YOU SCREAM, WE ALL SCREAM FOR ICE CREAM!

GOBBLING GARGOYLES GOBBLED GOBBLING GOBLINS.

HOW MUCH WOOD COULD CHUCK WOODS' WOODCHUCK CHUCK, IF CHUCK WOODS' WOODCHUCK COULD AND WOULD CHUCK WOOD? IF CHUCK WOODS' WOODCHUCK COULD AND WOULD CHUCK WOOD, HOW MUCH WOOD COULD AND WOULD CHUCK WOODS' WOODCHUCK CHUCK? CHUCK WOODS' WOODCHUCK WOULD CHUCK, HE WOULD, AS MUCH AS HE COULD, AND CHUCK AS MUCH WOOD AS ANY WOODCHUCK WOULD, IF A WOODCHUCK COULD AND WOULD CHUCK WOOD.

THE BOOK ON YOUR HEAD CHALLENGE

A SELF PORTRAIT

PUT YOUR POINTLESS 2 BOOK ON YOUR HEAD (NOT NOW, WAIT UNTIL YOU READ ALL THE INSTRUCTIONS FIRST!). GRAB A PEN AND DRAW THE FOLLOWING IMAGES ON THE PAGE WHILE HOLDING THE BOOK ON YOUR HEAD!

A FLOWER

POINTLESS FACTS

YOU BREATHE ON AVERAGE ABOUT FIVE MILLION TIMES A YEAR.

THE AVERAGE PERSON SPENDS TWO WEEKS OF THEIR LIFETIME WAITING FOR THE LIGHT TO CHANGE FROM RED TO GREEN.

YOUR LEFT LUNG IS SMALLER THAN YOUR RIGHT LUNG TO MAKE ROOM FOR YOUR HEART.

CHEWING GUM WHILE PEELING ONIONS WILL STOP YOU FROM CRYING.

THE OLDEST KNOWN GOLDFISH LIVED TO 43 YEARS OF AGE. HER NAME WAS TISH.

THE STRAW SOCCER GAME

LET'S PLAY SOME STRAW SOCCER! HERE'S HOW TO PLAY:

1. YOU'LL SEE THERE ARE TWO RECTANGLES ON THIS PAGE. CUT THEM OUT AND ROLL THEM LENGTHWAYS—THESE ARE YOUR STRAWS!

2. YOU'LL ALSO SEE THERE IS A CIRCLE ON THIS PAGE TOO. CUT THIS OUT AND ROLL IT INTO A BALL. THIS WILL BE YOUR, ERM, BALL!

3. ON THE PAGE OPPOSITE THERE ARE TWO GOALS. RIP THE PAGE OUT AND PLAY STRAW SOCCER WITH A FRIEND!

- - - - - - - - - - - - - - - - - -

CUT HERE

- - - - - - - - - - - - - - - - - -

CUT HERE

- - - - - - - - - - - - - - - - - -

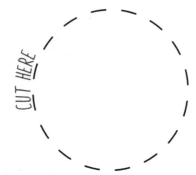

CUT HERE

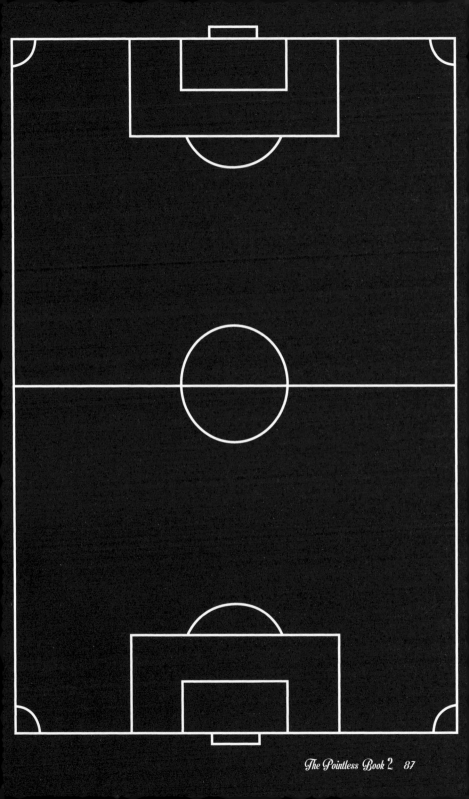

DESIGN YOUR LAPTOP BACK

DRAW AN AMAZING DESIGN ON THE BACK OF THE LAPTOP!

SODA PONG!

SCAN HERE TO SEE ALFIE'S ATTEMPTS

SODA PONG IS THE BEST GAME EVER.
FOR THIS GAME YOU WILL NEED:

1. A FRIEND

2. 12 PLASTIC CUPS

3. A PING PONG BALL " O "

4. A CARTON OF ORANGE JUICE

5. GRAVY MIX AND WATER (TO MAKE GRAVY!)

INSTRUCTIONS:

GRAB THE CUPS AND DIVIDE THEM INTO TWO GROUPS OF SIX.

IN SIX CUPS POUR A SPLASH OF ORANGE JUICE AND IN THE OTHER SIX ADD A SPLASH OF GRAVY.

MIX UP THE CUPS AND PLACE SIX AT ONE END OF A TABLE AND SIX AT ANOTHER END. THE AIM OF THE GAME IS TO BOUNCE THE PING PONG BALL INTO A CUP AND THE OPPONENT HAS TO DRINK WHATEVER IS IN THE CUP!

TWEETING RARITIES!

TWEET PICTURES TO #POINTLESSPICS WHEN YOU SEE THE FOLLOWING...

A WHITE PIGEON

ALFIE DEYES

A PINK CAR

A MAN ON A UNICYCLE

SOMEBODY WITH THE POINTLESS BOOK 2

A BRIGHT GREEN BUILDING

SOMEONE WITH POINTLESS BLOG MERCHANDISE

TO DO LIST

CATCHPHRASES

GUESS THE NAME OF THE SONG FROM
THE VISUAL CLUES BELOW...

1.

2.

_____

3.

4.

_____

SPECIAL BIRTHDAYS

NAME: _____

DATE: _____

WHAT DID YOU DO? _____

_____

NAME: _____

DATE: _____

WHAT DID YOU DO? _____

_____

NAME: _____

DATE: _____

WHAT DID YOU DO? _____

_____

NAME: _____

DATE: _____

WHAT DID YOU DO? _____

_____

WHAT ARE YOUR MOST PRIZED POSSESSIONS?

DRAW OR LIST THEM HERE:

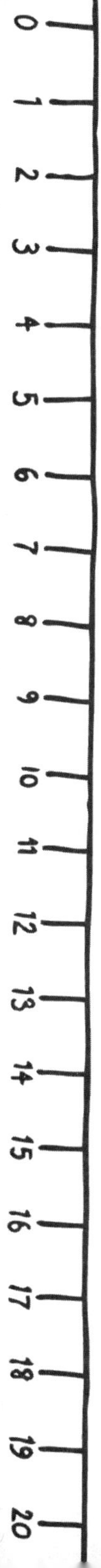
0
1
2
3
4
5
6
7
8
9
10
11
12
13
14
15
16
17
18
19
20

RULER REACTIONS

TEST YOUR REACTIONS USING YOUR VERY OWN POINTLESS BOOK 2! ASK A FRIEND TO HOLD THE BOOK LENGTHWAYS AND IN THE AIR. PLACE YOUR HANDS AROUND THE BOOK, BUT NOT TOUCHING IT. THE AIM IS TO CATCH THE BOOK AS SOON AS YOUR FRIEND DROPS IT AND TO MEASURE YOUR REACTIONS USING THE RULER ON THE BACK OF THE BOOK.

PERSONAL BESTS:

1. ____________CM

2. ____________CM

3. ____________CM

4. ____________CM

5. ____________CM

0–5	WAKEY! WAKEY! HAVE ANOTHER TRY...
6–10	SHARP, BUT NOT SHARP ENOUGH...
11–15	OK, THAT'S PRETTY IMPRESSIVE...
16–20	WOW! HELLO SPEEDY GONZALEZ!

PAINTING BY NUMBERS

PAINT THE PICTURE USING THE NUMBERS AND COLORS BELOW.

1. RED
2. ORANGE
3. YELLOW
4. PINK
5. LIGHT BLUE
6. DARK BLUE
7. BROWN
8. BLACK
9. GREEN
10. PURPLE

MAKE AN ALFIE FACE WITH YOUR FOOD...

EVERYONE LIKES PLAYING WITH THEIR FOOD! NOW YOU CAN PLAY WITH YOUR FOOD AND TWEET IT TO

#POINTLESSFOOD

MAKE ALFIE'S FACE OUT OF YOUR FAVORITE DINNER AND TWEET AWAY!

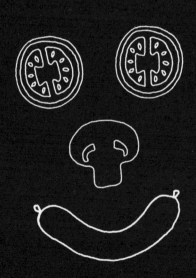

TREASURE HUNT

CREATE YOUR OWN TREASURE HUNT TO DO WITH YOUR FRIENDS! HIDE THIS BOOK SOMEWHERE SAFE AND WRITE DOWN CLUES FOR THEM TO FOLLOW IN ORDER TO FIND IT. KEEP HOLD OF CLUE ONE (THEY'LL NEED THAT TO START THE HUNT) AND HIDE THE REST IN DIFFERENT SPOTS FOR THEM TO FIND—REMEMBER, CLUE 1 SHOULD LEAD TO CLUE 2, AND SO ON!

CLUE 1

CLUE 2

CLUE 3

CLUE 4

CLUE 5

CREATE YOUR OWN CARTOON CHARACTER!

GRAB A PICTURE OF YOURSELF AND DRAW A CARTOON CHARACTER. EXAGGERATE YOUR FEATURES AND BE CREATIVE!

SCAN HERE TO SEE ALFIE'S CARTOON

DESIGN A T-SHIRT

HERE'S ANOTHER DESIGN ACTIVITY. ADD AN AMAZING DESIGN TO THE T-SHIRT BELOW; YOU CAN ADD WHATEVER YOU LIKE—JUST BE CREATIVE!

CREATE YOUR OWN ULTIMATE CHOCOLATE BAR!

EVERYONE LOVES CHOCOLATE. NOW'S YOUR CHANCE TO DESIGN YOUR VERY OWN CHOCOLATE BAR! WE'VE STARTED OFF THE DESIGN BELOW...

DREAM JOURNAL

LAST NIGHT I DREAMT: _____

_____

_____

_____

_____

_____

_____

_____

_____

_____

_____

_____

_____

_____

_____

_____

_____

I THINK THIS MEANS: _____

_____

_____

_____

_____

_____

CUT-OUT LOVEHEARTS

EVER WANTED TO TELL SOMEONE HOW YOU REALLY FEEL ABOUT THEM BUT NEVER KNEW WHAT TO SAY? NOW'S YOUR CHANCE! JUST DECORATE THE LOVEHEARTS BELOW, CUT THEM OUT AND PASS THEM ON.

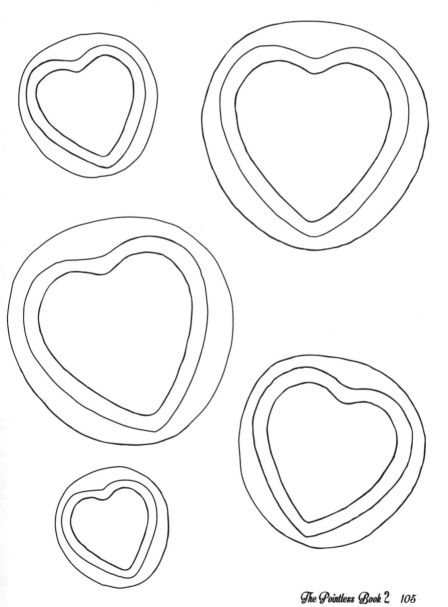

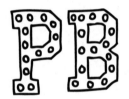

THE 'YES' AND 'NO' GAME

SCAN HERE TO SEE ALFIE'S ATTEMPTS

GRAB A FRIEND AND PLAY THE 'YES' AND 'NO' GAME.

HERE'S HOW TO PLAY:

PLAYER 1 THINKS OF A FAMOUS PERSON.

PLAYER 2 ASKS PLAYER 1 A SERIES OF QUESTIONS. PLAYER 1 HAS TO ANSWER THE QUESTIONS WITHOUT SAYING 'YES' OR 'NO'!

EACH PLAYER RECORDS THEIR TIME AND THE WINNER IS THE PLAYER WHO HAS LASTED THE LONGEST WITHOUT SAYING 'YES' OR 'NO'!

PLAYER 1	PLAYER 2

PIN THE TAIL ON NALA

EVERYONE REMEMBERS 'PIN THE TAIL ON THE DONKEY' FROM THEIR CHILDHOOD—SO LET'S PLAY A GAME OF 'PIN THE TAIL ON NALA'!

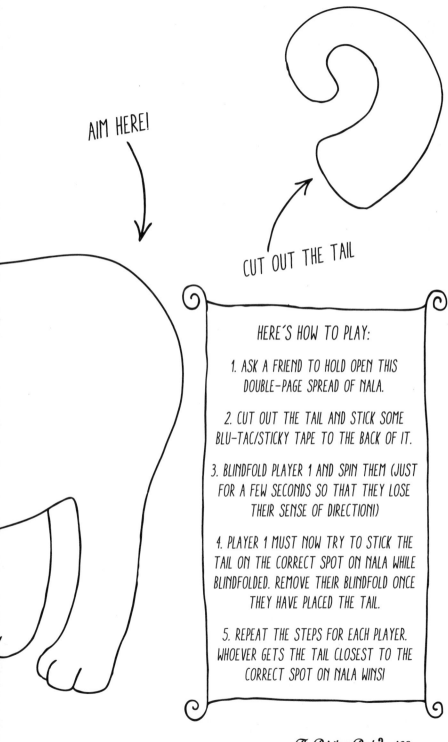

AIM HERE!

CUT OUT THE TAIL

HERE'S HOW TO PLAY:

1. ASK A FRIEND TO HOLD OPEN THIS DOUBLE-PAGE SPREAD OF NALA.

2. CUT OUT THE TAIL AND STICK SOME BLU-TAC/STICKY TAPE TO THE BACK OF IT.

3. BLINDFOLD PLAYER 1 AND SPIN THEM (JUST FOR A FEW SECONDS SO THAT THEY LOSE THEIR SENSE OF DIRECTION!)

4. PLAYER 1 MUST NOW TRY TO STICK THE TAIL ON THE CORRECT SPOT ON NALA WHILE BLINDFOLDED. REMOVE THEIR BLINDFOLD ONCE THEY HAVE PLACED THE TAIL.

5. REPEAT THE STEPS FOR EACH PLAYER. WHOEVER GETS THE TAIL CLOSEST TO THE CORRECT SPOT ON NALA WINS!

DESIGN YOUR OWN MENU

BREAKFAST

LUNCH

DINNER

DESSERT

MIRROR WRITING

CHECK OUT THE IMAGES BELOW. GRAB A MIRROR AND WRITE WHAT YOU SEE...

DO MORE OF WHAT MAKES YOU HAPPY!

NAIA IS THE COOLEST DOG IN THE WORLD!

SORRY ABOUT MY HAIR!

YOU DON'T HAVE TO DO WHAT EVERYONE ELSE IS DOING!

MAKE SOCK PUPPETS

OKAY POINTLESS PEOPLE, IT'S TIME TO GET CREATIVE
WITH YOUR, ERM, SOCKS!

WHAT YOU NEED:

ONE LONELY UNPAIRED SOCK
CRAFT GLUE
TWO BUTTONS FOR THE EYES
SOME WOOL

INSTRUCTIONS:

1. FIRST PUT THE SOCK ON YOUR HAND SO THAT
YOUR FINGERS ARE IN THE TOE SECTION AND YOUR
THUMB IS IN THE HEEL SECTION. MARK WHERE YOU'D
LIKE THE EYES TO BE.

2. NEXT, GLUE THE BUTTONS TO THE SOCK AT
THE POINTS WHERE YOU MARKED THE EYES.
(BE CAREFUL NOT TO SPILL ANY GLUE!)

3. NOW FOR THE HAIR! CUT THE WOOL INTO A COOL
HAIRSTYLE FOR YOUR PUPPET AND GLUE IT ON.

CONGRATULATIONS! YOU NOW HAVE YOUR VERY OWN SOCK PUPPET!

DRAW NALA'S BALL

NALA LOVES HER BALL; IT'S HER FAVORITE TOY. DESIGN NALA'S BALL IN THE SPACE BELOW, MAKING IT AS DECORATIVE AS YOU LIKE!

MAKE SURE YOU DRAW WITHIN THE LINES!

SCAN HERE TO SEE YOUR DESIGN

POINTLESS FLOWCHART

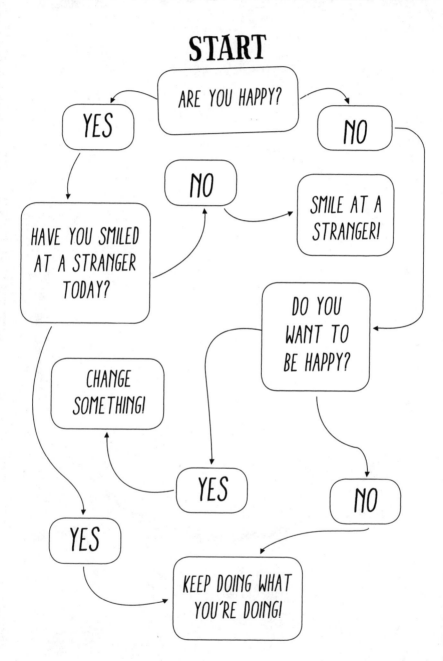

START

ARE YOU HAPPY?

YES

NO

NO

SMILE AT A STRANGER!

HAVE YOU SMILED AT A STRANGER TODAY?

DO YOU WANT TO BE HAPPY?

CHANGE SOMETHING!

YES

NO

YES

KEEP DOING WHAT YOU'RE DOING!

HIDE AND SEEK

GET YOUR FRIEND TO
HIDE YOUR BOOK AND
SEE HOW LONG IT TAKES
YOU TO FIND IT.

TIME:

DECORATE NALA'S BACKGROUND

THIS IS THE ULTIMATE CHALLENGE. COLOR IN NALA'S BACKGROUND!

WRITE DOWN YOUR TOP FIVE FAVORITE EVER TEXTS:

1. _____

_____

2. _____

_____

3. _____

_____

4. _____

_____

5. _____

_____

DRAW YOUR FAVORITE VIDEO OR FILM SCENE (COMIC BOOK STYLE)

GRATITUDE WEEK

WRITE DOWN SOMETHING YOU ARE GRATEFUL FOR
EVERY DAY OF THE WEEK.

MONDAY: _____

_____

_____

TUESDAY: _____

_____

_____

WEDNESDAY: _____

_____

_____

THURSDAY: _____

_____

_____

FRIDAY: _____

_____

_____

SATURDAY: _____

_____

_____

SUNDAY: _____

_____

_____

THE POINTLESS PRIZE PAGE!

EVERYONE DESERVES A PRIZE FROM TIME TO TIME. ON THIS PAGE, LIST
TEN REASONS WHY YOU DESERVE A POINTLESS PRIZE AND THEN WRITE
WHAT YOU THINK THAT PRIZE SHOULD BE!

1. _____

2. _____

3. _____

4. _____

5. _____

6. _____

7. _____

8. _____

9. _____

10. _____

THE PRIZE: _____

POINTLESS POETRY

YOU'RE A POET AND YOU KNOW IT! USE THE WORDS BELOW TO MAKE SOME POINTLESS POETRY! TWEET YOUR VERSE TO #POINTLESSPOETRY...

PUG
FUDGE
RAINBOW
CROISSANT
BUBBLE
CHEEKY
EMOJI
SUNSHINE
HAPPY
TOOTHPASTE
SMELLY
CHICKEN
MOONWALK
FIFTY
PEANUT
BUTTER
TWEET

ALFIE'S DICTIONARY CHALLENGE!

OK WORD WORMS, HERE IS A LIST OF OBSCURE WORDS.
TRY TO MATCH THEM WITH THE ANSWERS BELOW!

WORDS

1. BOONDOGGLE

2. CYGNET

3. GUMPTION

4. KALOOKI

5. OSCULATE

6. WIDDERSHINS

7. TALIPOT

8. HORNSWOGGLE

ANSWERS

A. TO CHEAT OR TRICK

B. COMMON SENSE

C. MOVE COUNTER CLOCKWISE

D. A YOUNG SWAN

E. A PALM TREE

F. A FORM OF RUMMY PLAYED
WITH TWO PACKS OF CARD

G. AN UNNECESSARY EXPERIENCE

H. TO KISS

THE POINTLESS PONDER PAGE

STOP HERE AND HAVE A THINK ABOUT THE FOLLOWING...

AT THE MOVIE THEATER, WHICH ARM REST IS YOURS?

IF AN AMBULANCE IS ON ITS WAY TO SAVE SOMEONE AND IT RUNS SOMEONE OVER, DOES IT STOP TO SAVE THEM OR CONTINUE TO THE FIRST PERSON?

ONE RAINDROP PLUS ANOTHER RAINDROP MAKES ONE RAINDROP?

WHY DOES A ROUND PIZZA COME IN A SQUARE BOX?

IF YOU PUT A CHAMELEON IN A ROOM FULL OF MIRRORS, WHAT COLOR WOULD IT TURN?

IF NOBODY BUYS A TICKET TO A MOVIE, DO THEY STILL SHOW IT?

DOES THE MAILMAN DELIVER HIS OWN MAIL?

WHY DOESN'T SUPERGLUE STICK TO THE INSIDE OF THE TUBE?

CHOOSE 5 WORDS BELOW
THAT BEST DESCRIBE YOU

FRIENDLY

KIND

AWKWARD

SILLY

FIERY

TALKATIVE

LOUD

CREATIVE

PRACTICAL

FRANTIC

LAZY

PROACTIVE

MUSICAL

SPORTY

TRUSTWORTHY

QUIET

GULLIBLE

FIDGETY

DREAMY

PERFECTIONIST

POSITIVE

INDEPENDENT

EMOTIONAL

LEADER

PARTICULAR

CANDID

OUTSPOKEN

HONEST

COMMITTED

KNOWLEDGEABLE

LOGICAL

COMPASSIONATE

CHEERFUL

PATIENT

FORGIVING

REBELLIOUS

UNDERSTANDING

ACHIEVER

THOUGHTFUL

QUIRKY

PERSISTENT

SOCIABLE

HARD WORKER

GENEROUS

FAVORITES

CHOOSE YOUR FAVORITE...

SWEET POPCORN OR SALTED POPCORN?

BIRTHDAY OR CHRISTMAS?

KITTENS OR PUPPIES?

PIZZA OR BURGER?

SUMMER OR WINTER?

TWITTER OR INSTAGRAM?

YOUTUBE OR TV?

NEW YORK OR PARIS?

SCAN HERE TO SEE ALFIE'S FAVORITES

FRUIT OR VEG?

SIX GLASSES ARE PLACED IN A ROW.

THE FIRST THREE CONTAIN WATER; THE SECOND THREE ARE EMPTY.

BY MOVING ONLY ONE GLASS, HOW IS IT POSSIBLE TO REARRANGE
THE GLASSES SO THEY ALTERNATE BETWEEN FULL AND EMPTY?

ANSWER: _____

_____

BEGINNING OF THE WEEK RESOLUTIONS

DATE: _____

RESOLUTION: _____

_____

_____

_____

DATE: _____

RESOLUTION: _____

_____

_____

_____

DATE: _____

RESOLUTION: _____

_____

_____

_____

DATE: _____

RESOLUTION: _____

_____

_____

_____

SPOT THE DIFFERENCE...

DOT TO DOT

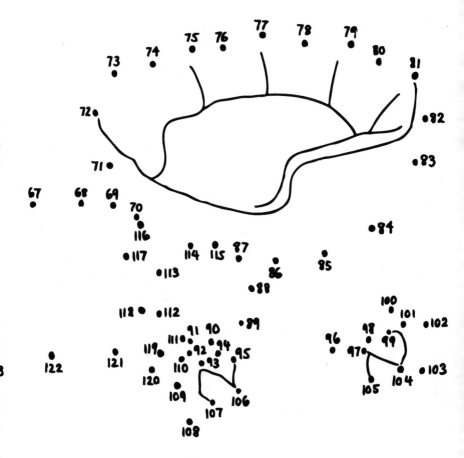

SPIN THE BOOK

GATHER SOME FRIENDS AND PLAY A GAME OF 'SPIN THE BOOK'. HERE'S HOW TO PLAY:

1. ON THE OPPOSITE PAGE WRITE A DARE IN EACH OF THE FIVE BOXES.

2. CUT OUT THE DARES.

3. CLOSE YOUR POINTLESS BOOK 2 (BUT READ ALL OF THE INSTRUCTIONS FIRST!).

4. SIT IN A CIRCLE WITH YOUR FRIENDS AND PLACE EACH DARE AROUND THE CIRCLE.

5. TURN OVER YOUR POINTLESS BOOK 2 AND LOOK FOR THE SPECIAL 'SPIN THE BOOK' ARROW.

6. TAKE IT IN TURNS TO SPIN YOUR POINTLESS BOOK 2.

7. IF THE ARROW STOPS ON A DARE, YOU HAVE TO PERFORM THE DARE.

8. IF IT MISSES A DARE, THEN THE BOOK IS PASSED ON TO THE NEXT PLAYER FOR THEIR TURN.

DARE 1

DARE 2

DARE 3

DARE 4

DARE 5

TABLE TENNIS

LET'S PLAY A GAME OF TABLE TENNIS—BUT WITH A TWIST.

HERE'S HOW TO PLAY:

1. YOU NEED AN OPPONENT SO GRAB A FRIEND WHO WOULD LIKE TO PLAY.

2. TEAR OUT THIS PAGE (NOT YET—READ ALL THE INSTRUCTIONS FIRST!).

3. SCRUNCH UP THE PAGE INTO A BALL. THIS IS YOUR PING PONG BALL.

4. CLOSE THE POINTLESS BOOK 2 AND PLACE IT ON ITS SIDE IN THE MIDDLE OF A TABLE (IF YOUR FRIEND HAS A POINTLESS BOOK 2 THEN YOU CAN USE THAT TOO!). THIS IS YOUR NET.

5. THE AIM OF THE GAME IS TO BOUNCE THE BALL OVER THE NET AND LAND IT ON THE OTHER SIDE OF THE TABLE.

6. THE WINNER IS THE PLAYER WHO SCORES THE MOST 'LANDINGS' AFTER TEN ATTEMPTS EACH.

CELEBRITY LINK GAME

THIS GAME IS SO MUCH FUN, ESPECIALLY IF YOU'RE TRYING TO PASS THE TIME. THE AIM OF THE GAME IS TO LINK CELEBRITIES USING THE FINAL LETTER OF THEIR NAMES. FOR EXAMPLE, EMMA WATSO<u>N</u> CAN BE LINKED TO <u>N</u>IALL HORA<u>N</u>, AND THEN <u>N</u>IALL HORA<u>N</u> CAN BE LINKED TO <u>N</u>ICKI MINA<u>J</u>... TRY IT WITH THE NAMES BELOW!

JUSTIN BIEBER

HARRY STYLES

GRAPH PAPER

FINISH THE TEXT CONVERSATION

'WAIT... SAID WHAT?!'

'I CAN'T BELIEVE HE ACTUALLY SAID THAT TO HER!!'

DOODLES

...FILL THIS PAGE WITH DOODLES!

GET YOUR FRIEND TO FILL THIS PAGE

PASS YOUR BOOK TO A FRIEND AND GET THEM TO FILL IN THIS PAGE

DRAW...

THE DESCRIPTION BELOW ON THE OPPOSITE PAGE AND SHARE USING #POINTLESSPICTURE...

ALFIE AND NALA WALKING ON THE MOON, ALONGSIDE A POINTLESS FLAG AND A POINTLESS SPACECRAFT. BE CREATIVE AND INCLUDE AS MUCH DETAIL AS YOU LIKE—SUCH AS A FEW STARS, THE SUN, EARTH, ANOTHER SPACECRAFT, A FEW ALIENS, A COUPLE OF METEORS, A FEW OF ALFIE'S FRIENDS, AND MAYBE EVEN A BLACK HOLE! DON'T FORGET TO TWEET YOUR PICTURE TO #POINTLESSPICTURE.

POINTLESS CHECKLIST

WRITE A CHECKLIST FOR TODAY AND TICK IT OFF AS YOU COMPLETE EACH ONE!

☐   ☐

☐   ☐

☐   ☐

☐   ☐

☐   ☐

☐   ☐

☐   ☐

☐   ☐

☐   ☐

☐   ☐

FAVORITE WEBSITES

_____

_____

_____

_____

_____

_____

_____

SPY ON PEOPLE

...WHAT DID YOU SEE?

STICK A CHILDHOOD PHOTO HERE

SCAN HERE TO SEE ALFIE'S PHOTO

ADD YOUR PHOTO WITHIN THE LINES

BEST EVER STATUSES

☐ _____
  _____

☐ _____
  _____

☐ _____
  _____

☐ _____
  _____

☐ _____
  _____

PALM READING

LET'S TRY SOME PALM READING AND SEE IF WE CAN LOOK INTO THE FUTURE...

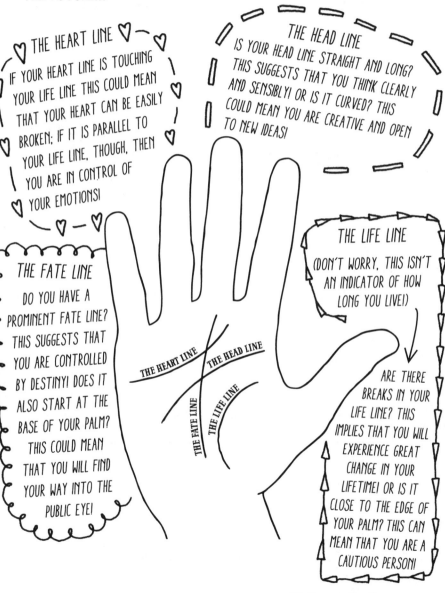

THE HEART LINE

IF YOUR HEART LINE IS TOUCHING YOUR LIFE LINE THIS COULD MEAN THAT YOUR HEART CAN BE EASILY BROKEN; IF IT IS PARALLEL TO YOUR LIFE LINE, THOUGH, THEN YOU ARE IN CONTROL OF YOUR EMOTIONS!

THE HEAD LINE

IS YOUR HEAD LINE STRAIGHT AND LONG? THIS SUGGESTS THAT YOU THINK CLEARLY AND SENSIBLY! OR IS IT CURVED? THIS COULD MEAN YOU ARE CREATIVE AND OPEN TO NEW IDEAS!

THE FATE LINE

DO YOU HAVE A PROMINENT FATE LINE? THIS SUGGESTS THAT YOU ARE CONTROLLED BY DESTINY! DOES IT ALSO START AT THE BASE OF YOUR PALM? THIS COULD MEAN THAT YOU WILL FIND YOUR WAY INTO THE PUBLIC EYE!

THE LIFE LINE

(DON'T WORRY, THIS ISN'T AN INDICATOR OF HOW LONG YOU LIVE!)

ARE THERE BREAKS IN YOUR LIFE LINE? THIS IMPLIES THAT YOU WILL EXPERIENCE GREAT CHANGE IN YOUR LIFETIME! OR IS IT CLOSE TO THE EDGE OF YOUR PALM? THIS CAN MEAN THAT YOU ARE A CAUTIOUS PERSON!

THE HEART LINE   THE HEAD LINE

THE FATE LINE   THE LIFE LINE

FUNNIEST OVERHEARD CONVERSATIONS ON A BUS OR A TRAIN

SECRET KEY

THIS WAY UP!

YOU'VE FOUND THE SECRET KEY!
NOW, CUT OUT THE SQUARE ON THE
DOTTED LINES AND FIND THE BOX
THAT NEEDS TO BE UNLOCKED...

RIP THIS PAGE...

...INTO PIECES AND STICK IT BACK TOGETHER TO MAKE THIS CIRCLE

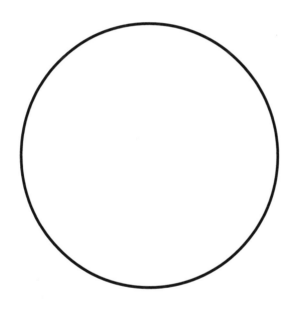

DRAW A COFFEE CUP

DESIGN YOUR COFFEE CUP IN THE SPACE BELOW, MAKING IT AS DECORATIVE AS YOU LIKE!

MAKE SURE YOU DRAW WITHIN THE LINES!

SCAN HERE TO SEE YOUR DESIGN

TIMELINE OF YOUR LIFE

USE THE LINE BELOW TO PLOT A TIMELINE OF YOUR LIFE.
BEGIN WITH YOUR DATE OF BIRTH AND BE AS CREATIVE AS
YOU WISH! YOU COULD EVEN PLOT INTO THE FUTURE...

ADD YOUR DATE OF
BIRTH HERE!

DRAW OR LIST ALL THE THINGS

SPRING

SUMMER

THAT REMIND YOU OF...

FALL

WINTER

CLOUD HUNTERS

TICK OFF THESE CLOUD TYPES
WHEN YOU SPOT THEM:

CIRROCUMULUS

☐ DATE: _____

CUMULONIMBUS

☐ DATE: _____

CIRRUS

☐ DATE: _____

ALTOCUMULUS

☐ DATE: _____

STRATOCUMULUS

☐ DATE: _____

STRATUS

☐ DATE: _____

NIMBOSTRATUS

☐ DATE: _____

TURN OFF THIS LIGHT

NOW HOW DO YOU

TURN IT BACK ON?

WRITE DOWN THE MOST EXCITING THINGS HAPPENING THIS YEAR

STICK ALL YOUR MOVIE TICKETS HERE AND RATE EACH FILM

☆☆☆☆☆

☆☆☆☆☆

☆☆☆☆☆

☆☆☆☆☆

☆☆☆☆☆

LIFE HACKS

CHECK OUT THESE AMAZING LIFE HACKS...

HERE'S HOW TO BUILD A SOFA FORT, JUST IN CASE YOU EVER NEED TO:

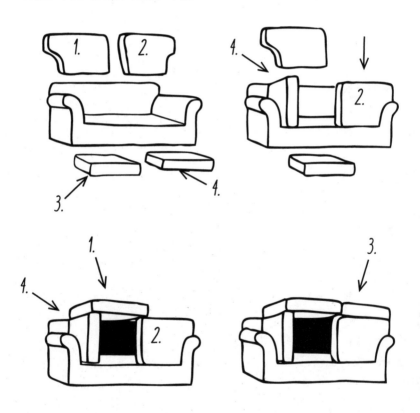

HOW TO MAKE AN ICE CREAM COOKIE SANDWICH:

YOU'LL NEED A TUB OF VANILLA ICE CREAM AND SOME COOKIES.

WITH A KNIFE*, CUT A SLICE OUT OF YOUR TUB.

GRAB YOUR COOKIES.

PLACE THE SLICE BETWEEN THE TWO COOKIES.

PEEL OFF THE TUB'S CARDBOARD...

...AND YOU HAVE AN ICE CREAM COOKIE SANDWICH!

HOW TO MAKE A HANDS-FREE POPCORN HOLDER:

WEAR A HOODIE BACK TO FRONT AND POUR IN YOUR POPCORN!

SCAN HERE TO SEE ALFIE IN ACTION

*ASK AN ADULT IF YOU ARE UNDER 16

POINTLESS PREDICTIONS FOR 2015

YOUR 3 PREDICTIONS:

1. _____
_____
_____
_____

2. _____
_____
_____
_____

3. _____
_____
_____
_____

YOUR FRIEND'S 3 PREDICTIONS:

1. _____
_____

_____
_____

2. _____
_____

_____
_____

3. _____
_____

_____
_____

GLUE HERE

LOCK THIS PAGE

...AND OPEN IT IN 12 MONTHS!

SECRET SWAPPING

WRITE DOWN A SECRET HERE AND SWAP
YOUR BOOK WITH A FRIEND TO SHARE THEM

MAKE THIS PAGE SPARKLY!

CUPCAKE FULL ENGLISH

SCAN HERE TO SEE ALFIE IN ACTION

CUPCAKES. BREAKFAST. TWO OF THE GREATEST THINGS IN THE WORLD! LET'S COMBINE THE TWO AND MAKE A SCRUMPTIOUS CUPCAKE FULL ENGLISH! HERE ARE THE INSTRUCTIONS:

1. PRE-HEAT THE OVEN TO 400°F.*

2. GRAB SOME BREAD AND A CUPCAKE TRAY.

3. DAB A LITTLE OIL INTO EACH CUP.

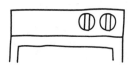

4. CUT THE BREAD INTO ENOUGH CIRCLES FOR YOUR TRAY AND PLACE IN EACH CUP.

5. MEANWHILE BROWN SOME BACON IN A FRYING PAN.*

6. WRAP THE BROWNED BACON AROUND THE INSIDE OF EACH CUP AND BAKE FOR 10 MINUTES.

7. SCRAMBLE SOME EGGS IN A SEPARATE DISH AND POUR INTO THE CUPCAKE TRAY HOLES. DON'T FORGET TO SPRINKLE SOME CHEESE TOO!

8. BAKE FOR ANOTHER 10 MINUTES UNTIL THE EGG IS SET AND THE CHEESE HAS MELTED.

9. ENJOY!

*ASK AN ADULT IF YOU ARE UNDER 16

DOUBLE BOOK SELFIE

OWN A COPY OF THE POINTLESS BOOK 1 AS WELL AS THE POINTLESS BOOK 2? THEN GRAB YOUR COPIES AND TAKE A POINTLESS BOOK SELFIE! TWEET TO

#POINTLESSBOOKSELFIE

DRAW OR LIST THINGS THAT MAKE YOU HAPPY!

DRAW YOUR FAVORITE YOUTUBER...

5 NEW FOODS

SCAN HERE TO REVEAL ALFIE'S CHOICES

TRY 5 FOODS YOU'VE NEVER TRIED BEFORE AND LIST THEM HERE. WHAT WAS EACH ONE LIKE?

1. _____
_____

2. _____
_____

3. _____
_____

4. _____
_____

5. _____
_____

CHUBBY BUNNY CHALLENGE

HERE'S A CLASSIC: THE CHUBBY BUNNY CHALLENGE. FOR THIS GAME YOU'LL NEED:

A PACKET OF MARSHMALLOWS.
MAYBE A COUPLE OF FRIENDS TO LAUGH AT YOU.

HERE'S HOW TO PLAY:

1. PUT A MARSHMALLOW IN YOUR MOUTH.

2. SAY `CHUBBY BUNNY`.

3. PUT ANOTHER MARSHMALLOW IN YOUR MOUTH.

4. SAY `CHUBBY BUNNY`.

5. PUT A MARSHMALLOW IN YOUR MOUTH.

6. SAY `CHUBBY BUNNY`.

7. PUT ANOTHER MARSHMALLOW IN YOUR MOUTH.

8. SAY `CHUBBY BUNNY`.

9. KEEP GOING UNTIL YOU CAN'T SAY `CHUBBY BUNNY`.

DO MORE OF WHAT MAKES YOU HAPPY

IF YOU HAD A PUG WHAT WOULD YOU CALL IT?

_____

TRUE OR FALSE?

	T	F
THE COLOR ORANGE IS NAMED AFTER THE FRUIT.	☐	☐
GOOGLE WAS ORIGINALLY CALLED 'BACKRUB'.	☐	☐
HUMAN HAIR AND FINGERNAILS CONTINUE TO GROW AFTER DEATH.	☐	☐
THERE ARE 86,400 SECONDS IN A DAY.	☐	☐
HUMANS SHARE 90% OF THEIR DNA WITH BANANAS.	☐	☐
IT IS IMPOSSIBLE TO BREATHE AND SWALLOW AT THE SAME TIME.	☐	☐

DRAW FROM MEMORY...

WITH A FRIEND, LOOK AT THE PICTURE BELOW FOR FIVE SECONDS AND COVER IT UP. TRY TO DRAW THE PICTURE FROM MEMORY ON THE OPPOSITE PAGE AND SEE WHO REMEMBERS THE MOST!

YOU

YOUR FRIEND

ANSWER PAGES

POINTLESS RIDDLES

PAGE 16

1. WIND

2. TWELVE! JANUARY 2ND; FEBRUARY 2ND ETC...

3. AN UMBRELLA

4. A WINDOW

TRANSLATION PAGE

PAGE 72

1. CHINESE

2. GERMAN

3. ITALIAN

4. GREEK

5. FRENCH

6. SPANISH

CATCHPHRASES

PAGE 92

1. SING BY ED SHEERAN

2. STEAL MY GIRL BY ONE DIRECTION

3. GHOST BY ELLA HENDERSON

4. HAPPY BY PHARRELL WILLIAMS

DICTIONARY CHALLENGE

PAGE 126

1 - G

2 - D

3 - B

4 - F

5 - H

6 - C

7 - E

8 - A

CUP RIDDLE

PAGE 130

BY ONLY MOVING THE SECOND GLASS, POUR THE WATER INTO THE FIFTH GLASS!

TRUE OR FALSE ANSWERS

PAGE 185

1. TRUE—THE FRUIT CAME BEFORE THE COLOR. BEFORE THE 16TH CENTURY THE COLOR ORANGE WAS REFERRED TO AS YELLOW-RED.

2. TRUE—THE SEARCH ENGINE BEGAN IN 1996 AND WAS CHANGED TO 'GOOGLE' IN 1997.

3. FALSE—GLUCOSE IS NEEDED FOR FINGERNAILS TO GROW, AND OXYGEN IS REQUIRED FOR HAIR GROWTH—BOTH OF WHICH DO NOT OCCUR IN THE BODY AFTER DEATH.

4. TRUE—60 SECONDS IN A MINUTE, 60 MINUTES IN A HOUR, 24 HOURS IN A DAY = 86,400!

5. FALSE—WE DO SHARE DNA BUT ONLY 50%.

6. TRUE—TRY IT!

SPOT THE DIFFERENCE

PAGE 132